I0468927

Table of Contents

INTRODUCTION

The Federal Communications Commission (FCC or Commission) is pleased to present its fiscal year (FY) 2017 budget request. The Commission requests $358,286,000 in budget authority from regulatory fee collections to carry out its core statutory mission and Congressional mandates. This represents a decrease of $25,726,497 million or 6.7 percent from the FY 2016 level of $384,012,497, of which $44,168,497 was specifically made available for the necessary expenses associated with moving to a new facility or reconfiguring the existing space to significantly reduce space consumption.

In FY 2017, the Commission requests the second installment of $16,866,992 for that same purpose. This represents the funds needed in FY 2017 to complete the move or reconfiguring of the existing space through the General Services Administration (GSA). This process is necessitated by the expiration of the FCC's current lease in October 2017. To move forward with the process, the FCC already secured oversight permission from the U.S. House of Representative Committee on Transportation & Infrastructure in July 2015, and the U.S. Senate Committee on Environment and Public Works in August 2015. Based on the current timeline, the award for the contract for the move or the reconfiguring of the existing space should be issued in the spring of 2016. The new contract will provide a more efficient utilization of space to reduce the Commission's footprint and also provides savings of up to $119 million over fifteen years through reduced rental costs.

The Commission also requests funds to follow through on essential information technology (IT) upgrades that includes rewriting legacy applications as part of a modular "shift" to a modern, resilient cloud-based platform. These IT modernization efforts will allow the Commission to support IT systems, including licensing and public safety, with less funds in the future. These requests provide the necessary funding to continue IT modernization projects that the Commission already invested significant resources in during prior fiscal years. With the necessary funding, the FCC expects to realize costs savings between $2 million and $3 million by the end of the modernization efforts and an additional $5 million to $10 million over the next five years.

The Commission made a concerted effort to curb the escalating IT operation and maintenance (O&M) costs back in FY 2014. Prior to FY 2014, the FCC faced ever-increasing costs in operating and maintaining its aging legacy IT systems. To counter these escalating O&M costs, the FCC IT team took the first bold step in early September 2015 by physically relocating over 200 different legacy servers from the FCC's headquarters in Washington, D.C. to a commercially hosted federal-certified facility located in West Virginia. These servers contained almost 400 different program applications. By physically relocating these servers to a commercially hosted provider, not only will O&M costs be reduced, but it will also allow for improved resiliency and a shift of many legacy applications to the cloud, similar to the Commission's Consumer Help Desk.

In FY 2014, 86 percent of IT funding was utilized for O&M and only 14 percent was utilized for development, modernization, and enhancements (DME). Those percentages are expected to change to 49 percent O&M and 51 percent DME by the end of FY 2017. The savings that will be realized on the O&M side will be redirected to delivering new capabilities.

The Commission initiated further efficiencies in its overall operations in FY 2015 through the following measures:

- Adopted an Order to realign the mission and resources of the Commission's Enforcement Bureau (EB) field offices. The final plan reflects feedback from wireless carriers, public safety entities, and broadcasters. The Order reduces the number of field locations, consolidates staff, and makes various other management and policy changes, including updating field equipment, requiring all field agents to have electrical engineering backgrounds and establishing procedures for industry and public safety complainants to escalate their complaints within the field organization. Savings from this realignment will be used to update equipment and employee skillsets.

- The current Commission headquarters offices that were housed in Portals I were consolidated into Portals II in FY 2015, which reduced the Commission's footprint by over 56,000 square feet and reduced rental payments by approximately $3 million. The savings realized in the Portals consolidation have been redirected to continue IT modernization.

- Initiated a review and evaluation of the Consumer and Government Affairs Bureau (CGB) call centers in Washington, DC and Gettysburg, Pennsylvania as result of efficiencies made in our Consumer Help Desk.

In addition, the Commission requests a transfer of $9,500,000 from the Universal Service Fund (USF) to the Commission to cover costs related to the oversight of the USF programs for the Enforcement Bureau and for the Office of Managing Director. Some of these funds will also be used to identify improvements to our current processes to identify, prevent, and detect improper payments in the USF programs.

In furtherance of these objectives and the FCC's mission, the FY 2017 budget request will be used to support the following Strategic Goals:

Strategic Goal 1: Promoting Economic Growth and National Leadership

Promote the expansion of competitive telecommunications networks which are a vital component of technological innovation and economic growth, helping to ensure that the U.S. remains a leader in providing its citizens opportunities for economic and educational development.

Strategic Goal 2: Protecting Public Interest Goals

The rights of network users and the responsibilities of network providers form a bond that includes consumer protection, competition, public safety and security. The FCC must protect and promote this Network Compact.

Strategic Goal 3: Making Networks Work for Everyone

In addition to promoting the development of competitive networks, the FCC must also ensure that all Americans can take advantage of the services they provide without artificial impediments.

Strategic Goal 4: Promoting Operational Excellence

Make the FCC a model for excellence in government by effectively managing the FCC's resources and maintaining a commitment to transparent and responsive processes that encourage public involvement and best serve the public interest.

In November 2015, Congress passed the Bipartisan Budget Act of 2015, which included Title X, the Spectrum Pipeline Act of 2015 (Act or Spectrum Pipeline Act). The Act requires the FCC to reallocate and auction 30 megahertz of spectrum identified by the Secretary of Commerce for reallocation from Federal use to non-Federal use, shared use, or a combination. The Act also appropriates funds from the Spectrum Relocation Fund to support activities by Federal entities to improve the efficiency and effectiveness of the Federal use of spectrum in order to make Federal spectrum available for non-Federal use, shared use, or a combination, and requires the FCC, as part of its role on the Technical Panel, to review Federal entities' proposals for funds for these purposes.

The Commission's FY 2017 budget submission includes a request for an increase in the cap on spending of spectrum auctions proceeds to $124.0 million, an increase of $7.0 million over FY 2016, in furtherance of the following objectives: making more spectrum available for commercial use, including executing the requirements mandated by Congress in the Spectrum Pipeline Act; administering the Television Broadcaster Relocation efforts for the incentive auctions; funding ongoing licensing as a result of successful auctions; planning for additional future auctions; and relocation of auction-related personnel and systems associated with the FCC Headquarters' move/restacking initiative.

As in prior years, the Commission is submitting details of its FY 2017 budget request at the organizational level to show the proposed use of budgetary resources. In addition, the Commission's budget request also shows the proposed use of budgetary resources by key activities within each bureau and office. We welcome the budgetary process and stand ready to provide Congress with the necessary information to ensure efficient and effective operation of the Commission.

Summary of Request

The FCC requests a FY 2017 appropriation of $358,286,000 from offsetting collections for Salaries and Expenses, which is a decrease of $25,726,497 from the FY 2016 appropriated level. In addition, the Commission requests a transfer of $9,500,000 from the Universal Service Fund (USF) to the Commission to cover costs related to the oversight of the USF programs. Some of these funds will also be used to identify improvements to our current processes to identify, prevent, and detect improper payments in the USF programs. Further, the FCC requests $124,000,000 in retained auction proceeds, which is an increase of $7,000,000 from the FY 2016 level in furtherance of making more spectrum available for commercial use and to implement the requirements mandated by Congress in the Spectrum Pipeline Act of 2015. From these resources, the projected full-time equivalents (FTEs) for Salaries and Expenses and auctions, combined, is 1,650.

The Commission will use FY 2017 resources to carry out its fundamental mission to ensure that the American people have available, at reasonable costs and without discrimination, rapid, efficient, Nation-wide and world-wide communications services whether by radio, television, wire, wireless, satellite, or cable.

(Dollars in Thousands)

	FY 2016		FY 2017		Change in Request	
	FTEs	Enacted	FTEs	Congressional Request	FTEs	Amount
Budget Authority - Offsetting Collections:						
Regulatory Fees - Commission	1,590	$372,412	1,590	$356,035	0	-$16,378
Regulatory Fees - Office of Inspector General (OIG)	60	$11,600	60	$11,751	0	$151
Subtotal - Offsetting Collections	**1,650**	**$384,012**	**1,650**	**$367,786**	**0**	**-$16,226**
Recovery of Universal Service Fund (USF) Oversight Cost	0	$0	0	-$9,500	0	-$9,500
Subtotal - Offsetting Collections & Recovery of USF Oversight Cost	**1,650**	**$384,012**	**1,650**	**$358,286**	**0**	**-$25,726**
Budget Authority - Other Offsetting Collections:						
Economy Act/Miscellaneous Other Reimbursables		$4,000		$4,000		$0
Auction Cost Recovery Reimbursement - Commission		$116,738		$123,735		$6,997
Auction Cost Recovery Reimbursement - OIG		$262		$265		$3
Subtotal - Other Offsetting Collections		**$121,000**		**$128,000**		**$7,000**
Subtotal: Offsetting Collections & Recovery of USF Oversight Cost	**1,650**	**$505,012**	**1,650**	**$486,286**	**0**	**-$18,726**
Other Budget Authority:[1]						
Credit Program Account		$100		$100		$0
Universal Service Fund Oversight - OIG		$1,685		$3,475		$1,790
Recovery of USF Oversight Cost - Commission		$0		$9,500		$9,500
Subtotal: Other Budget Authority		**$1,785**		**$13,075**		**$11,290**
Total Gross Proposed Budget Authority	**1,650**	**$506,797**	**1,650**	**$499,361**	**0**	**-$7,436**

[1] The Middle Class Tax Relief and Job Creation Act of 2012 (ACT) mandated that the Commission reimburse reasonable channel relocation costs incurred by those qualified TV Broadcasters that will be affected by the Incentive Auction The ACT also gave the Commission the authority to borrow up to $1 Billion from the Treasury and authorized the Commission to use an additional $750 million from Incentive Auction revenues to reimburse TV Broadcasters for relocation costs The TV Broadcaster Relocation Fund is capped at $1 75 Billion This budget authority is not represented in the above schedule to provide a better historical comparison of the components of the FCC's regular budgetary requests Information related to the ACT is presented in the Appendix section

Fiscal Year 2017 Proposed Appropriation Language

For necessary expenses of the Federal Communications Commission, as authorized by law, including uniforms and allowances therefore, as authorized by 5 U.S.C. §§ 5901-5902; not to exceed $4,000 for official reception and representation expenses; purchase and hire of motor vehicles; special counsel fees; and services as authorized by 5 U.S.C. § 3109, $341,419,008, to remain available until expended: *Provided*, That in addition, $16,866,992 shall be made available until expended for necessary expenses associated with moving to a new facility or reconfiguring the existing space to significantly reduce space consumption: *Provided further*, That $358,286,000 of offsetting collections shall be assessed and collected pursuant to section 9 of title I of the Communications Act of 1934, shall be retained and used for necessary expenses and shall remain available until expended: *Provided further*, That the sum herein appropriated shall be reduced as such offsetting collections are received during fiscal year **2017** so as to result in a final fiscal year **2017** appropriation estimated at **$0**: *Provided further*, That any offsetting collections received in excess of $358,286,000 in fiscal year **2017** shall not be available for obligation: *Provided further*, That remaining offsetting collections from prior years collected in excess of the amount specified for collection in each such year and otherwise becoming available on October 1, **2016**, shall not be available for obligation: *Provided further*, That, notwithstanding 47 U.S.C. § 309(j)(8)(B), proceeds from the use of a competitive bidding system that may be retained and made available for obligation shall not exceed $124,000,000 for fiscal year **2017**: *Provided further*, That, of the amount appropriated under this heading, not less than $11,751,073 shall be for the salaries and expenses of the Office of Inspector General: *Provided further, That,* in addition, $9,500,000 shall be transferred from the Universal Service Fund to the Commission in fiscal year **2017** to remain available until expended, to oversee the Universal Service Fund.

Legislative Proposals

The Administration is proposing legislative changes in the President's FY 2017 Budget that pertain to the FCC. These proposals are designed to improve spectrum management and represent sound economic policy.

Spectrum License Fee Authority

To promote efficient use of the electromagnetic spectrum, the Administration proposes to provide the FCC with new authority to use other economic mechanisms, such as fees, as a spectrum management tool. The FCC would be authorized to set charges for unauctioned spectrum licenses based on spectrum-management principles. Fees would be phased in over time as part of an ongoing rulemaking process to determine the appropriate application and level for fees.

Auction Domestic Satellite Service Spectrum Licenses

The FCC would be allowed to assign licenses for certain satellite services that are predominantly domestic through competitive bidding, as had been done before a 2005 court decision called the practice into question on technical grounds. The proposal is expected to raise $50 million from 2017–2026. These receipts would be deposited in the general fund for deficit reduction.

Auction or Assign via Fee 1675-1680 Megahertz

The Budget proposes that the FCC either auction or use fee authority to assign spectrum frequencies between 1675-1680 megahertz for flexible use by 2020, subject to sharing arrangements with Federal weather satellites. Currently, the spectrum is being used for radiosondes (weather balloons), weather satellite downlinks, and data broadcasts, and the band will also support future weather satellite operations. NOAA began transitioning radiosondes operations out of the band in 2016 as part of the Advanced Wireless Services 3 (AWS-3) relocation process. If this proposal is enacted, NOAA would establish limited protection zones for the remaining weather satellite downlinks and develop alternative data broadcast systems for users of its data products. Without this proposal, these frequencies are unlikely to be auctioned and repurposed to commercial use. The proposal is expected to raise $300 million in receipts over 10 years.

Summary of FYs 2015 – 2017 FTEs and Funding by Bureaus and Offices

(Dollars in Thousands)

Bureaus and Offices	FY 2015		FY 2016		FY 2017	
	FTEs	Actuals	FTEs	Enacted	FTEs	Congressional Request
Chairman and Commissioners	25	$4,689	23	$4,374	23	$4,431
Consumer & Government Affairs Bureau	156	$24,354	150	$23,365	145	$22,656
Enforcement Bureau	252	$44,937	240	$43,227	211	$45,390
International Bureau	113	$20,693	110	$20,735	111	$21,005
Media Bureau	171	$26,089	169	$25,009	175	$25,335
Public Safety & Homeland Security Bureau	101	$18,113	99	$18,590	101	$18,832
Wireless Telecommunications Bureau	212	$15,943	212	$15,909	216	$16,116
Wireline Competition Bureau	166	$30,248	164	$31,970	165	$32,386
Office of Administrative Law Judges	3	$357	3	$419	3	$424
Office of Communications Business Opportunities	11	$1,886	10	$1,636	10	$1,658
Office of Engineering & Technology	88	$15,207	87	$14,961	91	$15,156
Office of General Counsel	85	$15,741	79	$16,169	81	$16,379
Office of Legislative Affairs	12	$2,182	12	$1,980	12	$2,006
Office of Managing Director	206	$99,399	190	$146,533	201	$126,626
Office of Media Relations	16	$2,883	15	$2,809	15	$2,846
Office of Strategic Planning & Policy Analysis	25	$3,972	23	$4,134	26	$4,188
Office of Workplace Diversity	4	$654	4	$592	4	$600
Subtotal	**1,646**	**$327,347**	**1,590**	**$372,412**	**1,590**	**$356,035**
Office of Inspector General	38	$9,585	60	$11,600	60	$11,751
Subtotal	**1,684**	**$336,932**	**1,650**	**$384,012**	**1,650**	**$367,786**
Recovery of USF Oversight Cost	0	$0	0	$0	0	-$9,500
TOTAL	**1,684**	**$336,932**	**1,650**	**$384,012**	**1,650**	**$358,286**

FTEs - Historical & Estimated
Fiscal Years 1983 – 2017

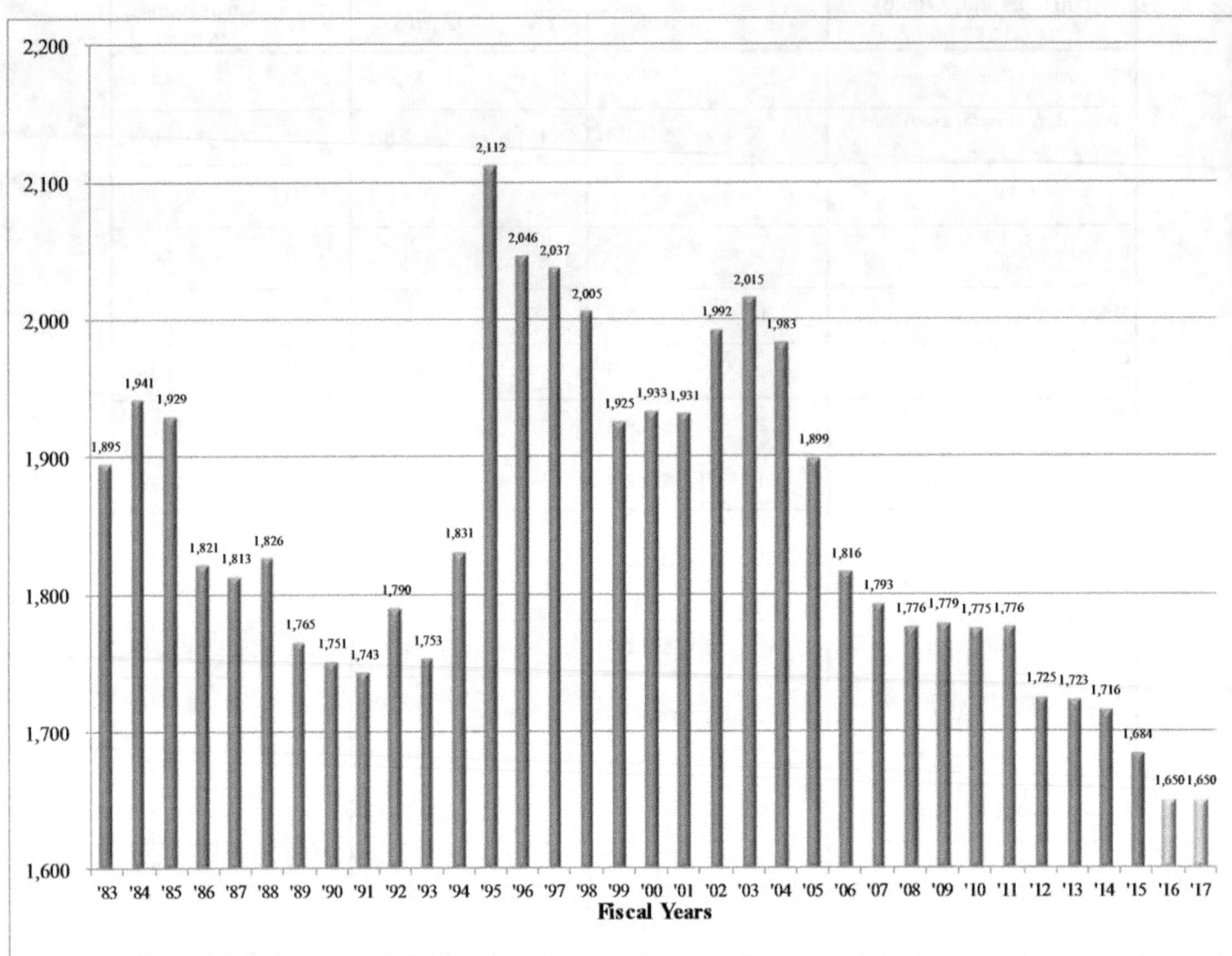

Fiscal years 2016 and 2017 are estimates.

Summary of Changes - Regulatory Fees (Offsetting Collections)

(Dollars in Thousands)

Offsetting Collections:	FY 2016 Enacted	FY 2017 Congressional Request	Net Change
Offsetting Collections - Commission	$372,412	$356,035	-$16,377
Offsetting Collections - Office of Inspector General (OIG)	$11,600	$11,751	$151
Total Spending Authority - Offsetting Collections	**$384,012**	**$367,786**	**-$16,226**
Recovery of USF Oversight Cost	$0	-$9,500	-$9,500
TOTAL NET CHANGE	**$384,012**	**$358,286**	**-$25,726**
Full-Time Equivalents (FTEs) - Commission	1,590	1,590	0
FTEs - Office of Inspector General	60	60	0
Total Full-Time Equivalents	**1,650**	**1,650**	**0**

Explanation of Changes

FY 2016 Appropriation - Offsetting Collections	**$384,012**
Reversal of FY 2016 New Initiative - Headquarters Move/Restack	-$44,168
FY 2017 Base Before Adjustments	**$339,844**
Salaries and Inflationary Increases to Base	
Commission	
Salary Increases - Pay Raises (1.3%)	$2,957
Non-Salary Increases (1.3%)[1]	$1,297
Office of Inspector General	
Salary Increases - Pay Raises (1.3%)	$112
Non-Salary Increases (1.3%)[1]	$39
Subtotal - Salaries and Inflationary Increases to Base	**$4,405**
Other Adjustments to Base	
IT - Geospatial Information System Solution	$400
One-Time Requests	
FCC Headquarters Move/Restacking	$16,867
IT - Rewriting of FCC Legacy Applications Phase II	$3,870
IT - Geospatial Information System Solution	$800
OMD - Targeted Investments to Reduce USF Improper Payments	$1,600
Subtotal - Other Adjustments to Base and One-Time Requests	**$23,537**
TOTAL OFFSETTING COLLECTIONS BEFORE RECOVERY OF USF OVERSIGHT COST	**$367,786**
Recovery of USF Oversight Cost	**-$9,500**
TOTAL OFFSETTING COLLECTIONS AFTER RECOVERY OF USF OVERSIGHT COST	**$358,286**
TOTAL NET CHANGE	**-$25,726**

[1]Utilized the FY 2016 inflationary pay raise rate.

Narrative Explanation of Changes - Salaries and Expenses

Salaries and Inflationary Increases to Base: $4,405,008

1. **Personnel Compensation and Benefits** - The request of $3,068,990 provides funds to cover the cost of 1.3% for FY 2017 pay raises, which includes the related increase for OIG that totals $111,563.

2. **Non-Salary Increases** - The request of $1,336,018 provides expected inflationary increases for space rentals (GSA and non-GSA facilities), phones, utilities, printing and reproduction services, contractual services, and supplies. The total non-salary increase includes the related increase for OIG that totals $39,510. This increase is developed using the same inflationary rate as Personal Compensation and Benefits.

FY 2017 New Initiatives - One-Time Requests: $23,136,992; Increase to Base: $400,000

1. **FCC Headquarters (HQ) Move/Restacking ($16,866,992)**

In FY 2016, Congress provided the funding for the first part of the headquarters move or restacking project. In the current FY 2017 Budget Request, the Commission is requesting the portion of the funding necessary to complete the project.

The Commission's current lease for Portals II at 445 12th Street SW, Washington, DC will expire in October 2017. Prior to this expiration date, the General Services Administration (GSA) will require the Commission to either move to a new facility or restack the existing facility, and as part of this process, reduce our square footage and lower our rental expense. If the Commission does not move or restack the building before the termination of the lease, GSA has informed the Commission that the new lease payments will increase by approximately $9 million per year, and the lessor could require a 20% premium over the current rental rate for any holdover period. It is estimated that the move or restacking will provide up to $119 million in total savings over fifteen years of the new lease.

GSA published the FCC's requirements for the new headquarters on FedBizOpps in July 2015. Based on the current timeline, the FCC expects to issue the lease for the new headquarters in the spring of 2016.

2. **IT Modernization ($4,670,000)**

   a. **Rewriting of FCC Legacy Applications as a Modular "Shift" to a Modern, Resilient Cloud-based Platform Phase II ($3,870,000)**

   Since many of the Commission's 207 IT systems contain applications that are more than a decade old, the software and code associated with the Commission's existing IT architectures are unable to support a move to a cloud-based infrastructure as they currently stand – they are simply too old to be hosted in a cloud-based platform. To accomplish these needed updates, the Commission's IT modernization plan includes an update to applications in a modular fashion in order to place them in the cloud structure while supporting continuing operations. The Commission will follow a three-part plan: (1) adapt open source solutions for Commission application needs where appropriate; (2) buy commercial software if adaption is not available or if a cost effective option is not available; and (3) create code if neither open source nor commercial options are available.

The applications will be redesigned and provided through a service catalog approach in a true cloud environment. This rewrite also provides an opportunity to simultaneously improve resiliency, security, and functionality. The replacement of the Commission's legacy infrastructure with a managed IT service provider will complete the "lift" away from the Commission's physical infrastructure – the rewriting of the Commission's legacy IT applications will complete the "shift" to a cloud-based platform. Some data can be moved readily to the cloud; however, existing applications with programmed logic must be recoded using agile methods that leverage open source and commercially available solutions wherever possible.

Moving to the cloud and rewriting applications within a cloud infrastructure enables the Commission to achieve an estimated long-term cost avoidance of $5 million to $10 million over five years in hardware and personnel/contractor costs. Transitioning to the cloud also accelerates the modernization of the Commission's infrastructure and improves the resiliency and security of the Commission's IT. This request will allow the Commission to continue the IT Modernization work efforts to align with government priorities to improve the security of cyber systems.

The following two charts show the heavy lift that the Commission has already performed and additional tasks that must be completed in modernizing its IT infrastructure. These investments will decrease the FCC's future operation and maintenance costs and those savings will be used to provide new capabilities.

FCC Modernization 3 Steps to Progress

1. Stabilization FY2014-2015
- Assessment
- Inventory
- Consolidation
- Server Move

2. Rationalization FY2015
- Software assessment
- Procure a platform
- Obtain stakeholder approval
- Deliver application roadmap to the cloud

3. Modernization FY2016-2018
- Universal Licensing System (ULS)
- NORS, DIRS, ETRS (Network Outage Reporting System and Disaster Reporting System)
- International Bureau Filing System (IBFS)
- Equipment Authorization System (EAS)
- Cable Operations Licensing System (COALS)
- Canadian Co-Channel Coordination System, (COSER)
- Consolidated Database System (CDBS)
- OET Frequency Assignment System (OFACS)
- Experimental Licensing System (ELS)
- Electronic Tariff Filing System (ETFS)
- OET Knowledge Database & Inquiry Processing System (OET KDB)

Cloud Solutions

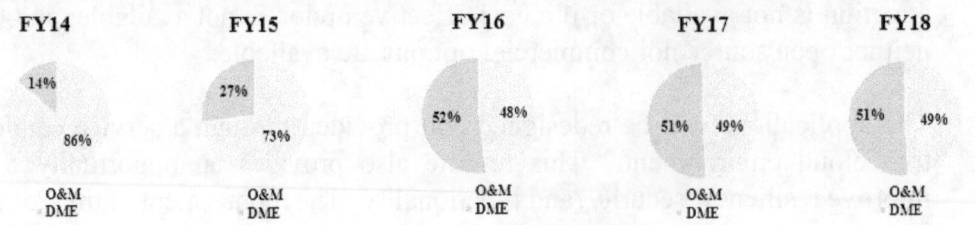

Investment in FCC IT Modernization Results in More Development (DME) Efforts Rather Than Legacy O&M

FY14	FY15	FY16	FY17	FY18
14% / 86%	27% / 73%	52% / 48%	51% / 49%	51% / 49%
O&M / DME	O&M / DME	O&M / DME	O&M / DME	O&M / DME

Shift in FCC IT spend from Legacy on-Premise to Cloud

- There is a very clear trend toward additional investment in cloud and shared services and less on maintaining legacy systems.
- The cost of modernization historically was dwarfed by the cost to maintain legacy systems in the out years, with O&M essentially meaning no new capability deliveries for the Bureaus and Offices.
- A roughly 50/50 O&M vs DME split is anticipated in FY18 and beyond. Note: these figures are reflective of FCC IT Spend, and do not include investments reported on behalf of Financial Operations, Universal Service Administrative Company, or Telecommunications Relay Service.

b. Geospatial Information System Solution (One-Time Request $800,000; Increase to Base $400,000)

Map visualization and geospatial analysis are becoming increasingly essential at the FCC. The collection of geospatial data through multiple FCC forms (e.g., 477 and Study Area Boundaries), and the need to display this information back to the public, have emphasized the need for a cloud-based enterprise Geospatial Information System (GIS) hosting solution. Moving to a cloud-based hosting solution provides several key benefits including consolidation of data, reduction of duplicative efforts and data, and increased system flexibility and capacity.

This request provides for migrating existing GIS solutions (e.g., FCC.gov/Maps) to a Cloud-Based GIS Hosting Solution. FCC.gov/Maps is one of the most highly trafficked sites for the Commission with over 338,000 unique visitors per year. Currently, the geospatial data is located in a variety of shared network drives and databases; much of it is on legacy infrastructure that is at or nearing its end of life. These data files are very large and are causing data storage capacity challenges. Additionally, the distributed geospatial web applications increase system complexity and result in unnecessary distribution and/or duplication of data sets.

The best option to address these challenges is to centralize the data into one modern cloud-based hosting solution that will keep the data organized, secured, and accessible for all FCC stakeholders. In addition, centralizing the data allows for increased transparency and interoperability across the FCC for all geospatial projects. Using a common repository, the FCC will also be able to create standardized geospatial data sets for commonly used data (e.g., Census). This improvement would allow FCC users to know where to download the data directly or have the ability to run their work on the server, thus eliminating duplicate data on shared networks and possibly eliminating redundant work. Additionally, this platform will allow for the creation of standard maps to accommodate the growing need of rapid release maps. This improvement will reduce the time spent on GIS development and standardize the way the maps appear. It will also allow for common features on each map, such as download options and base maps, resulting in a better user experience.

For GIS, the Commission is requesting a one-time amount of $800,000 for implementation and an increase to the base of $400,000 for continual operation and maintenance.

3. **Targeted Investments to Reduce USF Improper Payments ($1,600,000)**

The Commission and the Universal Service Administrative Company (USAC) are committed to collecting universal service contributions and disbursing payments to program beneficiaries that are accurate, timely, properly documented, and in compliance with rules established by the FCC. In furtherance of this commitment to integrity of the Universal Service Fund (USF), the FCC has directed USAC to develop two separate programs, the Beneficiary and Contributor Audit Program (BCAP) and Payment Quality Assurance (PQA) program.

BCAP is designed to measure rates of program compliance among universal service beneficiaries and contributors. In administering the BCAP, USAC utilizes audit approaches tailored to both the distinctive features of the participant's organization and the specific amounts of money being audited. The PQA Program complements the BCAP program and allows USAC to provide the FCC with information about improper payments to program beneficiaries, as required by the Improper Payments Information Act of 2002 (IPIA), the Improper Payments Elimination and Recovery Act of 2010 (IPERA), and the Improper Payments Elimination and Recovery Improvement Act (IPERIA) of 2012. Under the PQA program, USAC assesses specific payments made to select beneficiaries in required USF programs to determine if these payments were made in accordance with FCC rules. Using the results of these assessments, USAC calculates estimates of improper payment rates that the FCC then uses to inform its oversight and management of the USF as well as complying with annual Federal financial reporting requirements.

Since their inception, the BCAP and PQA programs have been useful in identifying improper payments and under-collections of contributions. Based on the results of the BCAP and PQA programs, the FCC has determined that the USF program would benefit from the implementation of technology to identify, detect, and prevent improper payments before they have an opportunity to occur. By applying predictive analytics to USF claims to identify abnormal or suspicious patterns prior to payments going out, the FCC believes that it can better limit improper payments and increase the effectiveness of its efforts to detect and prevent fraud. To achieve this goal, the FCC would plan to acquire and implement new analytic technology that would best meet the FCC's needs for applying predictive models to the highest risks in the USF program. As a practical matter, the FCC would use the tool first to examine past claims by beneficiaries to look for patterns of potential fraud or false claims from prior years. Utilizing the results of these historical reviews, the FCC would then be able to apply methodologies to current year claims to prevent improper payments in real time before they occur. The FCC will keep learning more as time goes on. Based on this continuous cycle of testing and the accompanying feedback loop, the FCC would have the ability to keep on fine tuning its methodologies for future billing cycles. If the FCC is able to successfully integrate such a tool into the USF claims process, the FCC would increase the effectiveness of its limited enforcement resources by detecting patterns of non-compliance with FCC rules in the program. Utilizing data analysis of this kind, the FCC's

Enforcement Bureau can more readily identify the participants in the USF system that may be knowingly or even willfully violating the rules to their advantage and thereby to the disadvantage of the USF system as a whole. The Enforcement Bureau may then increase the utility of its overall strategy to root out bad actors in the USF programs and take enforcement actions to deter others from engaging in similar activities. Furthermore, using this analysis, the FCC would also increase the flow of actionable information to its enforcement partners such as the Office of Inspector General and Department of Justice. Finally, over time, the FCC would expect that the cost of this system would yield a significant return on investment in terms of decreased improper payments and therefore making more funds available for the purposes that the USF programs are intended to serve.

Office of Inspector General Narrative

The Office of the Inspector General's (OIG) workload continues to increase in the areas of audit and investigation. Currently OIG only takes on top-level investigation cases and top risk finance and program audits. The Office keeps focus on increasing mission responsibility and ensuring appropriate staff levels to keep pace with the workload. The OIG Full Time Equivalent (FTE) staff has been increasing over the past few budget years and this influx has provided OIG more capability to maintain the mission of the OIG and assist with taking on more investigations and performing more audits.

The OIG FY 2017 budget request of $11,751,073 includes an inflation factor ($151,073) over the FY 2016 appropriated level of $11,600,000.

Over the next five years OIG Office of Audit (OA) plans include over 50 audits of Universal Service Fund Programs. This equates to 10 audits per year not including other financial and program audits. OIG OA currently has 13 active audits and 13 planned audits. OA audits have recovered approximately $2,478,134 in government funds over the last year. The audit reports are providing FCC management with critical findings necessary for sustaining the mission of the OIG.

The OIG Office of Investigation (OI) has 79 open cases. This is about the balance of cases open at any given time. For example, in the last fiscal year the OI received over 9,722 hotline contacts. OIG continues working with the Department of Justice (DOJ) and has recovered millions of dollars of government funds resulting from criminal cases referred to the DOJ. During the last fiscal year, OIG was instrumental in working with DOJ to recover $64,974,378 in government funds.

In compliance with the IG Reform Act of 2008 this FCC OIG FY 2017 budget request includes:

- A fair share ratio in the amount of $25,000 for contribution to the Council of the Inspectors General on Integrity and Efficiency (CIGIE),
- Funds to support IGNet Management Services, and,
- Training funds in the amount of $80,000.

Spectrum Auctions Program - Explanation of Requested Change

The Federal Communications Commission is requesting $124,000,000 for the Spectrum Auctions Program for FY 2017, as shown below.

(Dollars in Thousands)

	FY 2016		FY 2017		Requested Change	
	FTEs	Enacted	FTEs	Congressional Request	FTEs	Amount
Spectrum Auctions Cost Recovery	226	$117,000	230	$124,000	4	$7,000

Explanation of Changes	
FY 2016 Cap Level - Spectrum Auctions Program	**$117,000**
Reversal of FY 2016 New Initiatives - One-Time Requests	
FCC Headquarters Move/Restacking	-$7,190
TV Broadcaster Relocation Fund Administrator & Related Government Compliance Work	-$2,457
Subtotal	**-$9,647**
FY 2017 Base Before Adjustments	**$107,353**
Salaries and Inflationary Increases to Base	
Salary Increases - Pay Raises (1.3%)	$482
Non-Salary Increases (1.3%)[1]	$915
Subtotal - Salaries and Inflationary Increases to Base	**$1,397**
Other Adjustment to Base	
Additional FTEs Required to Enact the Spectrum Pipeline Act of 2015 (3)[2]	$580
IT Upgrades	
Auctions System Replacement	$3,500
Auction Warehouse	$300
Current Auction Implementations	
3.5 GHz Auction Development and Implementation	$1,750
ISAS Enhancements/Modifications	$1,500
Other Auction Development and Implementation	$1,000
Auction Security Enhancements	$875
Spectrum Pipeline Act Development	
SAS/ESC Testing for 3.5 GHz and Beyond	$1,250
Optimization for New Spectrum Opportunities	$1,250
Spectrum Visualization Tools - Public Facing and Internal	$500
Subtotal	**$12,505**
One-Time Requests	
FCC Headquarters Move/Restacking	$2,746
TOTAL REQUESTED - SPECTRUM AUCTIONS PROGRAM	**$124,000**
TOTAL CHANGE	**$7,000**

[1] Utilized the same inflationary rate as pay raises.
[2] Includes Benefits.

Spectrum Auctions Program

The Omnibus Budget Reconciliation Act of 1993, P.L. 103-66, required the Commission to auction portions of the spectrum for certain services, replacing the former lottery process. The Commission is required to ensure that small businesses, women, minorities, and rural telephone companies have an opportunity to participate in the competitive bidding process. The Commission initiated regulations implementing the spectrum auction authority granted by the legislation and conducted its first round of auctions in July 1994. To date the Commission has completed 87 auctions and the total amount collected for broader government use has exceeded $94.9 billion. The original spectrum auction authority was scheduled to expire in FY 1998; however, it was extended through FY 2007 in the Balanced Budget Act of 1997, P.L. 105-33; extended through FY 2011 by the Deficit Reduction Act of 2005, P.L. 109-171; extended through FY 2012 by the DTV Delay Act (2012), P.L. 111-4; extended through FY 2022, by the Middle Class Tax Relief and Job Creation Act of 2012, P.L. 112-96; and most recently, the authority was extended for specific purposes through FY 2025, by the Bipartisan Budget Act of 2015, P.L. 114-74.

The Commission is authorized to retain funds from auction revenues necessary to develop, implement, and maintain the auction program. These funds cover the personnel and administrative costs required to plan and execute spectrum auctions; operational costs to manage installment payments and collections activities; development, implementation, and maintenance of all information technology systems necessary for auctions operations, including development of a combinatorial bidding system; and a proportional share of the general administrative costs of the Commission based on the split of direct FTE hours. This budget submission assumes the auctions program will continue to recover the costs of conducting all auctions activities from spectrum license auction receipts as the Commission continues to use auctions as a licensing mechanism for spectrum-based communications services. The FY 2016 Appropriations language capped the auctions program at $117.0 million. The FCC is requesting $124.0 million for FY 2017 in large part to complete the necessary work required to modernize its auction IT systems and implement the Spectrum Pipeline Act of 2015 (Act or Spectrum Pipeline Act).

The Act requires the FCC to reallocate and auction 30 megahertz of spectrum identified by the Secretary of Commerce for reallocation from Federal use to non-Federal use, shared use, or a combination. The Act also appropriates funds from the Spectrum Relocation Fund to support activities by Federal entities to improve the efficiency and effectiveness of Federal use of spectrum in order to make Federal spectrum available for non-Federal use, shared use, or a combination, and requires the FCC, as part of its role on the Technical Panel, to review Federal entities' proposals for funds for these purposes. Additionally, the Act also requires the Commission to submit four separate reports to Congress. By November 2018, the Commission must submit a report on an analysis of its new rules for the innovative Citizens Broadband Radio Service in the 3550-3650 MHz band, and a report analyzing proposals to promote and identify additional bands that can be shared and identify at least 1 gigahertz of spectrum between 6 GHz and 57 GHz for such use. By January 1, 2022, the Commission must submit a report, in coordination with the Assistant Secretary of Commerce for Communications and Information, that identifies at least 50 megahertz of spectrum below 6 GHz for potential auction. Finally, by January 2, 2024, the Commission must submit a report, in coordination with the Assistant Secretary of Commerce for Communications and Information, that identifies at least an additional 50 megahertz of additional spectrum below 6 gigahertz for potential auction. Both of these latter two reports must contain an assessment of the Federal operations in such spectrum, an estimated timeline for the competitive bidding process, and a proposed plan for balance between unlicensed and licensed use.

As a result of the spectrum provisions included in the Spectrum Pipeline Act, the Congressional Budget Office scored auction proceeds at $4.42 billion for the period from FY 2016 through FY 2025. These upfront investment cost requests are less than one percent of the total revenue scored by the Congressional Budget Office.

The requested funding for FY 2017 is necessary to enable the Commission to continue ongoing auction activities as well as execute the mandates set forth by the Congress in the Spectrum Pipeline Act, including initiating the critical ground work necessary for the following items:

- Auctions Systems Replacement ($3,500,000). The replacement of 10-year-old old backend database and software components that support the auction application set-up and management. Modernization of this system is critical to conform to current best practices, allow for modular builds, communicate with auction bidding systems and other Commission databases, and enable greater flexibility for future auction development. This modernization will support all future auctions.

- 3.5 GHz Auction Development and Implementation ($1,750,000). These auctions will have a unique set of requirements, which includes auctioning more than 500,000 licenses every three years, at a minimum.

- Other Auction Development and Implementation ($1,000,000). The Commission needs to make additional changes to the auction bidding system for other planned auctions that include an AWS-3 re-auction, millimeter wave auction(s), FM Auction 83, and FM Translators.

- Auction Security Enhancements ($875,000). As recent news headlines have emphasized, the threat of cyber-attacks and security vulnerabilities are very real, and the Commission takes these threats and vulnerabilities very seriously. The FCC will proactively engage security engineers and architects to ensure the modernization of systems in the cloud are secure and adhere to Federal mandates and regulations to include two factor authentication. Making FCC auction systems resilient to cyber-attacks and mitigating security vulnerabilities will be a critical part of these efforts.

- SAS/ESC Testing for 3.5 GHz and Beyond ($1,250,000). The Spectrum Access System (SAS)/Environmental Sensing Capability (ESC) are necessary components to share additional spectrum, and are necessary to protect incumbent Federal operations. These systems will first be launched for the 3.5 GHz band, and may have additional applications in the future. Because the systems will work as a dynamic frequency coordinator for millions of devices, we need to ensure they operate properly and consistently with our rules prior to approval.

- Optimization for New Spectrum Opportunities ($1,250,000). The optimization team will help us analyze and study options for making new spectrum available, including through sharing scenarios, to ensure we are maximizing the amount of useful commercial spectrum.

They will develop optimal band plans accommodating incumbent uses and demonstrate the value of additional clearing or sharing as necessary.

- Spectrum Visualization Tools - Public Facing and Internal ($500,000). The public has a significant interest in understanding who has the rights to different spectrum bands at different locations, and desires the ability to manipulate and analyze this data. Federal agencies would also benefit from this information as they consider sharing/relocation options. Additionally, it is critical for internal teams to have robust data, including mapping, to understand coverage and operations across the country.

- Integrated Spectrum Auctions System (ISAS) Enhancement/Modifications ($1,500,000). It is necessary to modify the application forms for participation in each auction in response to the auction's unique requirements. This work will provide additional modernization of the primary auctions application via the ability to customize the form to support each auction.

- Auction Warehouse ($300,000). The Commission will create a persistent data warehouse where it will host the vast amounts of data generated from each auction. Keeping the data over time will help as both a reference and a tool to continue to improve the auctions and bidding systems.

The Balanced Budget Act of 1997, P.L. 105-33, required that the Commission provide to authorizing committees a detailed report of obligations in support of the auctions program for each fiscal year of operation, as a prerequisite to the continued use of auctions receipts for the costs of all auctions activities. As required by the law, each year the FCC provides the spectrum auctions expenditures report for the preceding fiscal year to Congress by the statutory deadline of September 30 of the following fiscal year. The following table shows available auction cash for the respective fiscal years.

Spectrum Auctions Activities

Fiscal Years 2010 - 2015

Dollars in Thousands

	2010	2011	2012	2013	2014	2015
Beginning Cash Balance as of October 1	$86,739	$217,280	$199,151	$166,489	$69,071	$317,931
Current Year Net Cash	164,049	23,581	(18,801)	(90,057)	252,796	11,115,179
Less:						
Deferred Revenue as of September 30[1]	(33,210)	(41,412)	(13,136)	(6,760)	(3,318)	(10,919,416)
Deposit Liability - Refunds as of September 30[2]	(298)	(298)	(725)	(601)	(618)	(238)
Available Cash as of September 30	**$217,280**	**$199,151**	**$166,489**	**$69,071**	**$317,931**	**$513,456**

[1]Cash associated with licenses that have not been granted as of stated date.

[2]Upfront auction deposits not refunded as of stated date.

Summary of Distribution of Resources - Spectrum Auctions Program

(Dollars in Thousands)

Object Classification Description	FY 2015 Actuals	FY 2016 Enacted	FY 2017 Congressional Request
Personnel Compensation & Benefits:			
Full-time & Other than full-time Permanent (11.1 & 11.3)	$27,040	$28,850	$29,678
Personnel benefits (12.0)	7,740	8,184	8,418
Sub-Total Personnel Compensation & Benefits	**$34,780**	**$37,034**	**$38,096**
Other Expenses:			
Benefits for former personnel (13.0)	$8	$11	$11
Travel & transportation of persons (21.0)	320	525	531
Transportation of things (22.0)	7	8	8
Rent payments to GSA (23.1)	6,708	6,090	6,169
Communications, utilities, & misc. charges (23.3)	1,423	1,512	1,532
Printing and reproduction (24.0)	209	174	177
Other services from non-Federal sources (25.2)	14,699	22,837	26,718
Other goods & services from Federal sources (25.3)	567	5,757	2,770
Operation & maintenance of equipment (25.7)	40,754	41,216	46,127
Supplies and materials (26.0)	556	248	252
Equipment (31.0)	745	1,583	1,604
Land and structures (32.0)	0	0	0
Insurance claims & indemnities (42.0)	4	5	5
Sub-Total Other Expenses	**$66,000**	**$79,966**	**$85,904**
Total Auctions Cost Recovery Reimbursable Authority:	**$100,780**	**$117,000**	**$124,000**

Spectrum Auctions Expenditures Report

Section 309(j) of the Communications Act permits the Commission to utilize funds raised from auctions to fund auction purchases, including contracts for services, and personnel performing work in support of Commission auctions authorized under that section. The FCC's Office of General Counsel (OGC) and Office of Managing Director (OMD) provide direction to FCC employees attributing hours for this purpose. The House of Representatives and Senate Appropriations Committees review and set a yearly cap for the spectrum auctions program. The requested cap level for FY 2017 is $124,000,000 in furtherance of making more spectrum available for commercial use and to implement the requirements mandated by Congress in the Spectrum Pipeline Act of 2015. This request is an increase of $7,000,000 from the FY 2016 cap level of $117,000,000.

The Commission's spectrum auctions expenditures support efficient licensing while also contributing funds to the U.S. Treasury and providing direct support to other broader government programs. In particular, in the Middle Class Tax Relief and Job Creation Act of 2012, Congress directed that proceeds from certain spectrum auctions, including auctions of licenses covering spectrum offered in the H-Block, AWS-3, and Incentive Auctions, fund certain public safety related programs and contribute to deficit reduction. Specifically, Congress directed that the net proceeds from these auctions be distributed as follows: $135 million for a state and local FirstNet implementation fund, $7 billion for FirstNet build out, $115 million for 911, E911, and NG911 implementation, $300 million for public safety research, and $20.4 billion plus any additional proceeds for deficit reduction.

The FCC has transferred $18.6 billion to the Public Safety Trust Fund to fund the state and local FirstNet implementation, the FirstNet buildout, and part of the public safety research program. The amount transferred to the Public Safety Trust Fund also includes $12.6 billion for deficit reduction. The AWS-3 auction included repurposed Federal spectrum that Federal agencies either relocated from or will be sharing with AWS-3 licensees. As required, a portion of the proceeds from the auction were deposited into the Spectrum Relocation Fund to support Federal agency relocation and/or sharing. The FCC deposited $11.5 billion into the Spectrum Relocation Fund from the AWS-3 auction for this purpose.

As of September 30, 2015, the Commission has raised more than $94.9 billion in auctions revenues since initiating the program in 1994. During this period, the auctions expenses have been less than two percent of the Commission's total auctions revenues. The Commission operated the auctions program for 10 years under a cap without any inflationary adjustments, only receiving increases in FYs 2013 through 2016 to fund the implementation costs for the incentive auctions and to fund the necessary expenses associated with moving to a new facility or reconfiguring the existing space to significantly reduce space consumption.

Spectrum auctions activities are performed agency-wide and are Information Technology (IT) intensive, as reflected in our Spectrum Auctions Expenditures Reports, which are provided to Congress on an annual basis. For example, the Incentive Auction team is composed of staff from across the Commission, including the Wireless Telecommunications Bureau, Media Bureau, International Bureau, Office of Engineering and Technology, Office of the Managing Director, and

Office of General Counsel. Auctions funds also cover the program's share of Commission operating expenses. The FCC uses these funds to enable successful auctions and expends them in a manner consistent with that objective.

In the practice of cost accounting, costs are identified as one of the following: (1) direct cost, (2) indirect cost, or (3) generally allocated cost. The methodology for deriving the proportional share of generally allocated administrative costs to be charged to the auctions program is based on the Commission's time reporting system and Generally Accepted Accounting Principles. The allocation is based on the percentage of actual hours that employees worked to support the auction program plus the same proportional share of the employee's indirect hours (leave hours). This full time equivalent (FTE) rate is applied to costs that benefit the Commission as a whole. These items that are allocated by the FTE rate include Commission-wide information technology systems, guard service, administrative facility services, supplies, furniture, equipment, and human resources training activities. The FCC has maintained an average of 14 percent for this purpose, with minor deviations.

In FY 2015, the Commission conducted two spectrum auctions: the Advanced Wireless Services (AWS-3) licenses auction of 65 megahertz of spectrum in the 1695-1710 MHz, 1755-1780 MHz, and 2155-2180 MHz bands that netted a total of $41.3 billion and an auction of 29 FM Broadcaster Construction Permits that netted $4.1 million.

Although the Commission is engaged in planning for a number of future auctions, the Commission's primary auctions focus in 2016 is on implementing the incentive auction process, in which bidding is currently scheduled to begin on March 29, 2016. The creation and adoption of rules and procedures for this first-ever two-sided auction of spectrum by the government has been substantially completed. The design and development of critical software to implement the incentive auction, which involves two separate but interdependent auctions – a reverse auction, which will determine the price at which broadcasters will voluntarily relinquish their spectrum usage rights, and a forward auction, which will determine the price the carriers are willing to pay for flexible use of wireless licenses, are also largely completed. The linchpin joining the reverse and the forward auctions is the "repacking" process. Repacking involves reorganizing and assigning channels to the remaining broadcast television stations in order to create contiguous blocks of cleared spectrum suitable for flexible use. The repacking component of this auction makes it uniquely, computationally complex, requiring additional software, cloud computing resources, and the assistance of skilled computer scientists, software engineers, and technology security experts. The design and development of those resources, which are critical to the implementation of the auction, is ongoing but largely complete.

Given the level of interest in the incentive auctions, with the involvement of both the broadcast and wireless communities, and the novelty and uniqueness of the auction, intense efforts in FYs 2016 and 2017 will be related to administering the auction process, including accepting and reviewing reverse and forward auction applications; developing and conducting bidder training and outreach; accepting and reviewing final applications for winning bidders in both the forward and reverse auctions; monitoring and supporting the bidding process; disbursing auction proceeds to winning bidders in the reverse auction; issuing licenses to winning wireless bidders and modifying licenses for broadcasters who are changing channels or voluntarily changing bands; and terminating licenses for those who voluntarily choose to cease broadcasting. Finally, staff must design and manage the repacking and transition process for clearing the appropriate portions of the band of broadcast licenses so it can be repurposed for broadband use.

The window for the reverse auction applications opened on December 8, 2015 and closed on January 12, 2016. Prior to the start of the reverse auction application window, the Commission engaged in a number of educational efforts to broadcasters. An online tutorial on the reverse auction application was made available, and additional tutorial segments will be added to walk broadcasters through the bidding process and the post-auction procedures. Also, an application process workshop was held to cover information related to the pre-auction process. During this workshop, participants were given the opportunity to ask questions following the presentation and appropriate FCC contact information was provided for any additional follow-up questions.

The window for the forward auction applications opened on January 27, 2016 and will close on February 10, 2016. Prior to the window for forward auction applications, the Commission conducted education and outreach efforts to familiarize potential forward auction bidders with new rules for competitive bidding that will affect the information collected on auction applications, including holding a webinar, posting an online tutorial, and providing detailed instructions for completing the application. As with the reverse auction, additional tutorial segments will be added to walk prospective bidders through the forward auction bidding process. The Commission has also released specifications for Auction System data file formats for the clock phase of the forward auction.

In January 2016, the Commission also launched a new website to serve as a repository of information on the broadcast incentive auction. The new website includes a range of materials that explains why the Commission is conducting the incentive auctions, how these auctions will benefit the public, and how the process works from end-to-end. The website provides information to educate consumers about what they will need to do to enjoy the over-the-air television stations once the auction has concluded. The new website features a section on "Frequently Asked Questions" for consumers, a calendar of key dates and events, and a "Resources" page where the public can easily access decisions and documents on the incentive auction. For potential participants in the incentive auction, the new website also provides a link to the FCC's broadcast incentive auction page where they can easily find needed resources such as the application form, tutorials, and other related information. This new website will also serve as a key component of the Commission's post-auction consumer education efforts to enhance a smooth transition for over-the-air TV viewers.

In addition, the Commission continues to plan for future auctions, including the re-auction of certain AWS-3 licenses, the auction of a number of FM allocations, and the creation of a new auction for Citizens Broadband Radio Service (CBRS) licenses. The CBRS auctions will involve over 500,000 licenses and will take place every three years, at a minimum. The Commission is also working to update and modernize its overall auctions system to be prepared to quickly hold new auctions when additional spectrum is made available.

Finally, the global race is on for so-called "5G" technologies and services, and the Commission is positioned to help ensure the United States will maintain its leadership in wireless through this transition. The Commission is bracing for this challenge by recently adopting a notice of proposed rulemaking proposing rules for four bands above 24 GHz for future wireless broadband services. Although the technology is still in development, the Commission is creating a flexible space in which these technologies can evolve, take hold, and explode across the U.S. The Commission's "spectrum frontiers" proceeding proposes to authorize 3,850 megahertz of spectrum for mobile and other services on a flexible use basis.

The demand for spectrum continues to grow, and making licenses available for new use through auctions is therefore one of the Commission's highest priorities. In addition to executing this mission in coordination with Federal agencies, the Congress has also set the mandates for providing more spectrum for non-Federal use, and the Commission is embracing those challenges. To execute the mandates set forth by Congress in the first-ever incentive auction and in the Spectrum Pipeline Act, and to develop and implement requirements for the wireless technologies of the future, additional resources are critical to maintaining the talent pool already at the Commission and for attracting new thinkers for tomorrow's wireless technologies. The Commission also needs additional resources to develop new or improve our auctions information technology infrastructure to sustain the planned spectrum auctions in the future. These small investments made now will provide great returns in the future as evidenced by the Congressional Budget Office scoring auction proceeds related to the Spectrum Pipeline Act at $4.42 billion for the years from FY 2016 through FY 2025.

The estimated FTE levels for the spectrum auctions program for FYs 2015 through 2017 are shown below.

FTEs by Resource Category

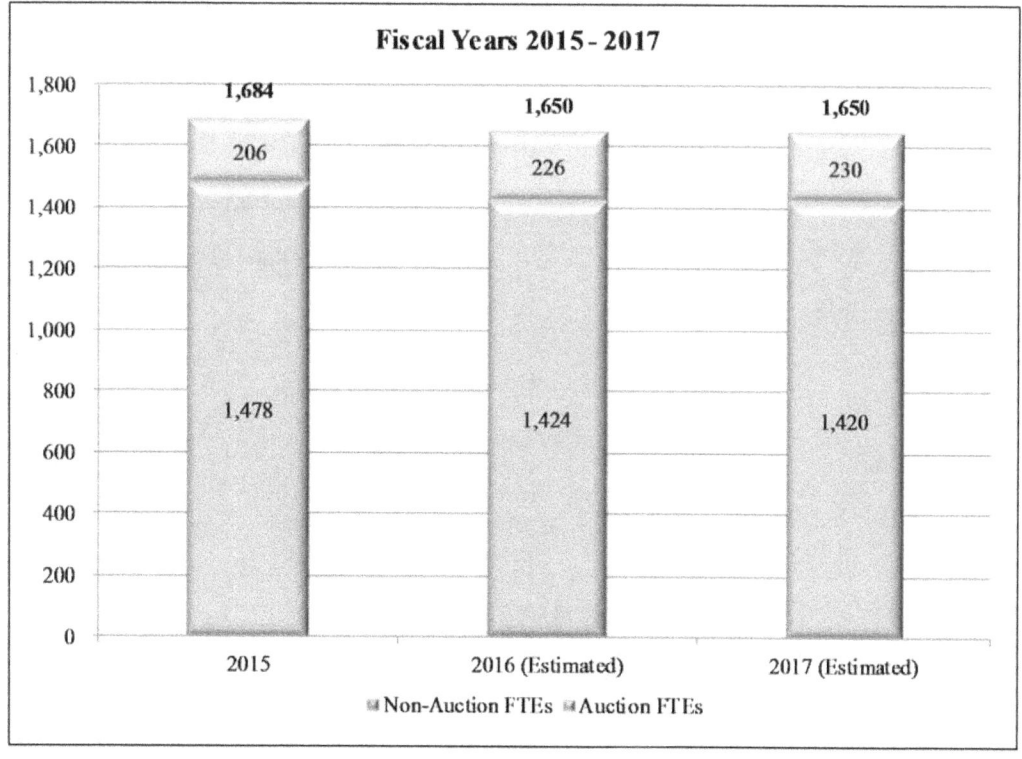

Spectrum Auctions and Collections
Fiscal Years 1994 through 2015
As of September 30, 2015

Fiscal Year	Number of Auctions	Number of Licenses Won	Amount Collected
1994	2	604	$652,954,213
1995	2	129	8,234,321,194
1996	6	2,026	2,019,376,024
1997	4	1,614	2,205,922,232
1998	2	1,388	860,878,576
1999	6	1,693	499,598,445
2000	8	4,403	1,335,043,185
2001	4	3,447	583,599,901
2002	7	7,036	135,630,842
2003	7	3,144	77,121,620
2004	5	267	126,790,232
2005	6	2,803	2,208,332,556
2006	5	1,284	13,834,972,696
2007	5	293	163,429,971
2008	3	1,144	18,987,705,659
2009	2	115	5,597,028
2010	3	4,788	25,972,328
2011	3	126	31,491,503
2012	1	93	3,869,571
2013	2	3,197	5,775,135
2014	2	186	1,564,594,550
2015	2	1,713	41,344,729,025
Totals	**87**	**41,493**	**$94,907,706,486**

Spectrum Auctions – Collections vs. Expenditures
Fiscal Years 1994 through 2015
(Dollars in Millions)

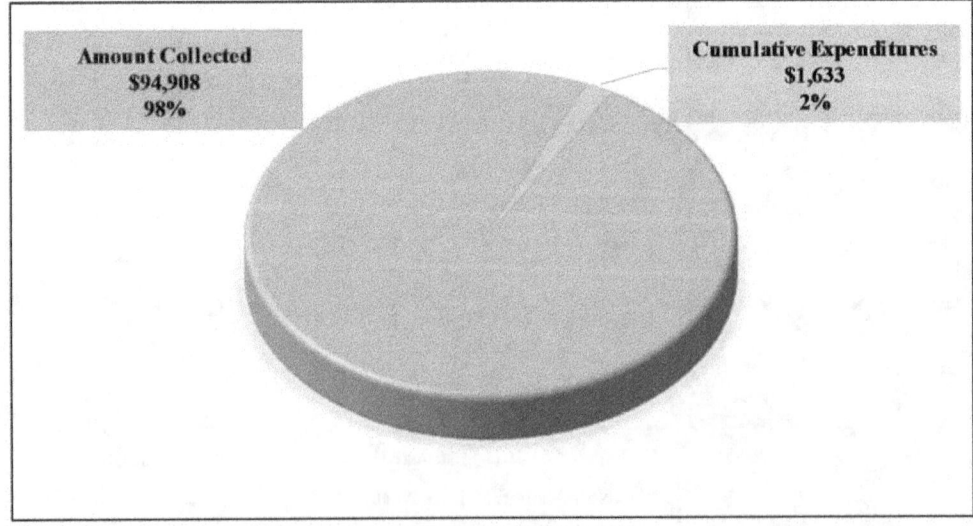

Cumulative Expenditures includes the amount appropriated for FY 2016.